Acknowledgments
We would like to thank all those who have given us
permission to include quotations in this book. Every
effort has been made to trace and acknowledge
copyright holders. We apologize for any errors or
omissions that may remain, and would ask those
concerned to contact the publishers, who will ensure
that full acknowledgment is made in the future.
Text
Extracts from the Authorized Version of the Bible (The
King James Bible), the rights in which are vested in the
Crown, are reproduced by permission of the Crown's
Patentee, Cambridge University Press.
'Now the green blade riseth' by J.M.C. Crum from *The
Oxford Book of Carols* © Oxford University Press 1928.
Artwork
Artwork by Amanda Barlow
Photographs
Photographs supplied by The Bodleian Library, University
of Oxford. Cover pictures: MS Douce 311, folio 122;
MSS Douce 219–220, folio 98. Inside pictures: MS
Rawl. liturg. f 26, folio 92v; MS Douce 311, folio 44;
MS Douce 14, folio 129v.

A catalogue record for this book is
available from the British Library
Printed and bound in Singapore

To Flo & Helen
With thanks for
your time in
Castle Donington
God Bless You
Tom & Pam Pegg

July 1998

THE GIFT OF EASTER
SEASON OF HOPE

LION
Giftlines

INTRODUCTION

The Easter story, in all its drama and passion, is like no other. After the death of Jesus, and the extraordinary events that surrounded it, nothing could ever be the same again—either for the group of ordinary and extraordinary people who were its principal players, or for the millions of people who have lived since then.

As we remember the events of the passion, and the true message of Easter unfolds, may it once again bring its precious message of hope, new life and new beginnings.

The angel said: 'He is not here: for he is risen, as he said. Come, see the place where the Lord lay.'

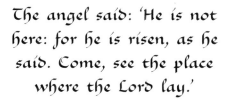

FROM MATTHEW'S GOSPEL

CONTENTS

THE DRAMA BEGINS

AND THEY BROUGHT THE COLT TO JESUS, AND CAST THEIR GARMENTS ON HIM; AND HE SAT UPON HIM.

AND MANY SPREAD THEIR GARMENTS IN THE WAY: AND OTHERS CUT DOWN BRANCHES OFF THE TREES, AND STRAWED THEM IN THE WAY. AND THEY... CRIED, SAYING, HOSANNA; BLESSED IS HE THAT COMETH IN THE NAME OF THE LORD:

BLESSED BE THE KINGDOM OF OUR FATHER DAVID, THAT COMETH IN THE NAME OF THE LORD: HOSANNA IN THE HIGHEST. AND JESUS ENTERED INTO JERUSALEM.

the king of peace

Rejoice greatly, O daughter of Zion; shout O daughter of Jerusalem: behold, thy King cometh unto thee: he is just, and having salvation; lowly, and riding upon an ass, and upon a colt the foal of an ass.

The prophet Zechariah, writing some five hundred years before these events, foretells Jesus' ride into Jerusalem. In Old Testament times, it was appropriate for kings to ride on asses for peaceful occasions. Horses were associated with war.

the hour is come

and it came to pass, when jesus
had finished all these sayings,
he said unto his disciples,
ye know that after two days is
the feast of the passover, and
the son of man is betrayed to
be crucified...

and jesus answered them,
saying, the hour is come, that
the son of man should be
glorified.

verily, verily, i say unto you,
except a corn of wheat fall
into the ground and die, it
abideth alone: but if it die, it
bringeth forth much fruit.

Now the green blade riseth from
the buried grain,
Wheat that in the dark earth
many days has lain;
Love lives again, that with the
dead has been:

Love is come again,
Like wheat that springeth green.

In the grave they laid him, Love
whom men had slain,
Thinking that never he would
wake again,
Laid in the earth like grain that
sleeps unseen:

Love is come again,
Like wheat that springeth green.

J.M.C. CRUM

the plot

THEN ASSEMBLED TOGETHER the
chief priests, and the scribes, and
the elders of the people... and
consulted that they might take
jesus by subtilty, and kill him.

THEN ONE OF THE TWELVE,
called judas iscariot, went unto
the chief priests,

and said unto them, what
will ye give me, and i will
deliver him unto you? and they
covenanted with him for thirty
pieces of silver.

and from that time he
sought opportunity to betray
him.

ThIRTY PIECES OF SILVER

And I said unto them, If ye think good, give me my price; and if not, forbear. So they weighed for my price thirty pieces of silver.

Zechariah's prophecy mentions exactly the amount that Judas required for his betrayal of Jesus.

the last supper

and when the hour was come, he [jesus] sat down, and the twelve apostles with him.

and he said unto them, with desire i have desired to eat this passover with you before i suffer...

and as they did eat, he said, verily i say unto you, that one of you shall betray me.

and they were exceeding sorrowful, and began every one of them to say unto him, lord, is it i?

MATTHEW 26:26–28, 30

BREAD AND WINE

AND AS THEY WERE EATING, JESUS
TOOK BREAD, AND BLESSED IT, AND
BRAKE IT, AND GAVE IT TO THE
DISCIPLES, AND SAID, TAKE, EAT;
THIS IS MY BODY.

AND HE TOOK THE CUP, AND
GAVE THANKS, AND GAVE IT TO
THEM, SAYING, DRINK YE ALL OF IT;

FOR THIS IS MY BLOOD OF THE
NEW TESTAMENT, WHICH IS SHED
FOR MANY FOR THE REMISSION OF
SINS.

AND WHEN THEY HAD SUNG AN
HYMN, THEY WENT OUT INTO THE
MOUNT OF OLIVES.

GETHSEMANE

THEN COMETH JESUS WITH THEM
UNTO A PLACE CALLED GETH-
SEMANE... AND HE TOOK WITH HIM
PETER AND THE TWO SONS OF
ZEBEDEE, AND BEGAN TO BE
SORROWFUL AND VERY HEAVY.

THEN SAITH HE UNTO THEM, MY
SOUL IS EXCEEDING SORROWFUL,
EVEN UNTO DEATH: TARRY YE HERE,
AND WATCH WITH ME.

AND HE WENT A LITTLE
FARTHER, AND FELL ON HIS FACE,
AND PRAYED, SAYING, O MY FATHER,
IF IT BE POSSIBLE, LET THIS CUP
PASS FROM ME: NEVERTHELESS NOT
AS I WILL, BUT AS THOU WILT.

JUDAS

AND WHILE HE YET SPAKE, LO,
JUDAS, ONE OF THE TWELVE, CAME,
AND WITH HIM A GREAT MULTITUDE
WITH SWORDS AND STAVES, FROM
THE CHIEF PRIESTS AND ELDERS OF
THE PEOPLE... AND FORTHWITH HE
CAME TO JESUS, AND SAID, HAIL,
MASTER; AND KISSED HIM.

ON TRIAL

AND THEY THAT HAD LAID HOLD ON JESUS LED HIM AWAY TO CAIAPHAS THE HIGH PRIEST...

AND THE HIGH PRIEST... SAID UNTO HIM, I ADJURE THEE BY THE LIVING GOD, THAT THOU TELL US WHETHER THOU BE THE CHRIST, THE SON OF GOD.

JESUS SAITH UNTO HIM, THOU HAST SAID: NEVERTHELESS I SAY UNTO YOU, HEREAFTER SHALL YE SEE THE SON OF MAN SITTING ON THE RIGHT HAND OF POWER, AND COMING IN THE CLOUDS OF HEAVEN.

THEN THE HIGH PRIEST RENT HIS CLOTHES, SAYING, HE HATH

spoken blasphemy; what further need have we of witnesses?

When the morning was come... [they] bound him, [and] led him away, and delivered him to Pontius Pilate the governor.

And Jesus stood before the governor: and the governor asked him, saying, art thou the king of the Jews? And Jesus said unto him, thou sayest...

Pilate saith unto them, what shall I do then with Jesus which is called Christ? They all say unto him, let him be crucified.

And the governor said, why, what evil hath he done? But they cried out the more, saying, let him be crucified.

THE SUFFERING SERVANT

He is despised and rejected of men; a man of sorrows, and acquainted with grief: and we hid as it were our faces from him; he was despised, and we esteemed him not.

Surely he hath borne our griefs, and carried our sorrows: yet we did esteem him stricken, smitten of God, and afflicted.

But he was wounded for our transgressions, he was bruised for our iniquities: the chastisement of our peace was upon him; and with his stripes we are healed.

All we like sheep have gone astray; we have turned every one to his own way; and the Lord hath laid on him the iniquity of us all.

The prophet Isaiah's vision of the Messiah as a man of sorrows gives a startlingly perceptive picture of the meaning of the cross.

CRUCIFIXION

AND WHEN THEY WERE COME UNTO
A PLACE CALLED GOLGOTHA... THEY
CRUCIFIED HIM, AND PARTED HIS
GARMENTS, CASTING LOTS.

AND SITTING DOWN THEY
WATCHED HIM THERE;

AND SET UP OVER HIS HEAD
HIS ACCUSATION WRITTEN, THIS IS
JESUS THE KING OF THE JEWS.

See from his head,
his hands, his feet,
Sorrow and love
flow mingled down;
Did e'er such love
and sorrow meet,
Or thorns compose
so rich a crown?

ISAAC WATTS

abandoned

and about the ninth hour Jesus cried with a loud voice, saying, Eli, Eli, lama sabachthani? that is to say, my God, my God, why hast thou forsaken me?

a psalm of rejection

My God, my God, why hast thou forsaken me? Why art thou so far from helping me, and from the words of my roaring?

In this moment of extreme desolation, Jesus prays the words of Psalm 22 in his own birth-tongue, Aramaic.

through the veil

jesus, when he had cried again with a loud voice, yielded up the ghost.

and behold, the veil of the temple was rent in twain from the top to the bottom...

The veil was the heavy curtain separating the inner court of the Temple from the Holy of Holies, where God dwelt. The violent removal of this barrier symbolized the opening of the way for sinners to approach God, through the 'torn' body of Jesus.

LAID TO REST

WHEN THE EVEN WAS COME, THERE
CAME A RICH MAN OF ARIMATHÆA,
NAMED JOSEPH, WHO ALSO HIMSELF
WAS JESUS' DISCIPLE:

He went to pilate, and
begged the body of jesus... he
wrapped it in a clean linen
cloth,

and laid it in his own new
tomb, which he had hewn out in
the rock: and he rolled a great
stone to the door of the
sepulchre, and departed.

A RICH MAN'S GIFT

And he made his grave with the wicked, and with the rich in his death; because he had done no violence, neither was any deceit in his mouth.

Joseph's action fulfilled this prophecy from the book of Isaiah.

DAWN

IN THE END OF THE SABBATH, AS IT
BEGAN TO DAWN TOWARD THE FIRST
DAY OF THE WEEK, CAME MARY
MAGDALENE AND THE OTHER MARY
TO SEE THE SEPULCHRE.

AND, BEHOLD, THERE WAS A
GREAT EARTHQUAKE: FOR THE ANGEL
OF THE LORD DESCENDED FROM
HEAVEN, AND CAME AND ROLLED
BACK THE STONE FROM THE DOOR,
AND SAT UPON IT.

HIS COUNTENANCE WAS LIKE
LIGHTNING, AND HIS RAIMENT WHITE
AS SNOW...

AND THE ANGEL... SAID UNTO THE WOMEN, FEAR NOT YE: FOR I KNOW THAT YE SEEK JESUS, WHICH WAS CRUCIFIED.

HE IS NOT HERE: FOR HE IS RISEN, AS HE SAID. COME, SEE THE PLACE WHERE THE LORD LAY.

AND GO QUICKLY, AND TELL HIS DISCIPLES THAT HE IS RISEN FROM THE DEAD; AND, BEHOLD, HE GOETH BEFORE YOU INTO GALILEE; THERE SHALL YE SEE HIM.

the tomb is empty

then she [mary] runneth, and
cometh to simon peter, and to
the other disciple, whom jesus
loved, and saith unto them,
they have taken away the lord
out of the sepulchre, and we
know not where they have laid
him... so they ran both
together: and... stooping down,
and looking in, saw the linen
clothes lying... and the napkin,
that was about his head, not
lying with the linen clothes, but
wrapped together in a place by
itself... [they] saw, and believed.

MARY MAGDALENE

THE FIRST DAY OF THE WEEK
COMETH MARY MAGDALENE EARLY,
WHEN IT WAS YET DARK... [SHE]
STOOD WITHOUT AT THE SEPULCHRE
WEEPING: AND AS SHE WEPT, SHE
STOOPED DOWN, AND LOOKED INTO
THE SEPULCHRE,

AND SEETH TWO ANGELS IN
WHITE SITTING, THE ONE AT THE
HEAD, AND THE OTHER AT THE FEET,
WHERE THE BODY OF JESUS HAD
LAIN.

AND THEY SAY UNTO HER,
WOMAN, WHY WEEPEST THOU? SHE
SAITH UNTO THEM, BECAUSE THEY

have taken away my lord, and i
know not where they have laid
him.

and when she had thus said,
she turned herself back, and
saw jesus standing, and knew
not that it was jesus.

jesus saith unto her,
woman, why weepest thou?
whom seekest thou? she,
supposing him to be the
gardener, saith unto him, sir, if
thou have borne him hence, tell
me where thou hast laid him,
and i will take him away.

jesus saith unto her, mary.
she turned herself, and saith
unto him, rabboni [my great
master]...

THE RISEN MASTER

AFTER THAT HE APPEARED IN
ANOTHER FORM UNTO TWO OF
THEM, AS THEY WALKED, AND WENT
INTO THE COUNTRY.

AND THEY WENT AND TOLD IT
UNTO THE RESIDUE: NEITHER
BELIEVED THEY THEM.

THEN THE SAME DAY AT
EVENING... WHEN THE DOORS WERE
SHUT WHERE THE DISCIPLES WERE
ASSEMBLED FOR FEAR OF THE JEWS,
CAME JESUS AND STOOD IN THE
MIDST, AND SAITH UNTO THEM,
PEACE BE UNTO YOU...

AND MANY OTHER SIGNS TRULY
DID JESUS IN THE PRESENCE OF HIS
DISCIPLES, WHICH ARE NOT WRITTEN
IN THIS BOOK:

BUT THESE ARE WRITTEN, THAT
YE MIGHT BELIEVE THAT JESUS IS
THE CHRIST, THE SON OF GOD; AND
THAT BELIEVING YE MIGHT HAVE LIFE
THROUGH HIS NAME.

BUT NOW IS CHRIST RISEN FROM THE DEAD, AND BECOME THE FIRSTFRUITS OF THEM THAT SLEPT.

FOR SINCE BY MAN CAME DEATH, BY MAN CAME ALSO THE RESURRECTION OF THE DEAD.

FOR AS IN ADAM ALL DIE, EVEN SO IN CHRIST SHALL ALL BE MADE ALIVE.

Paul writes this triumphant repudiation of the final power of death in his letter to the Corinthian church.

We think that Paradise
and Calvary,
Christ's Cross, and Adam's tree,
stood in one place;
Look Lord, and find both
Adams met in me;
As the first Adam's sweat
surrounds my face,
May the last Adam's blood
my soul embrace.

JOHN DONNE

EPILOGUE

I [JOHN]... WAS IN THE SPIRIT ON THE LORD'S DAY, AND [I SAW]... ONE LIKE UNTO THE SON OF MAN, CLOTHED WITH A GARMENT DOWN TO THE FOOT... HIS HEAD AND HIS HAIRS WERE WHITE LIKE WOOL... AND HIS EYES WERE AS A FLAME OF FIRE... AND HIS VOICE AS THE SOUND OF MANY WATERS... AND WHEN I SAW HIM, I FELL AT HIS FEET AS DEAD. AND HE LAID HIS RIGHT HAND UPON ME, SAYING UNTO ME, FEAR NOT; I AM THE FIRST AND THE LAST:

I AM HE THAT LIVETH, AND WAS DEAD; AND, BEHOLD, I AM ALIVE FOR EVERMORE...

Christ has risen from the dead,
by death defeating death,
and those buried in the grave
he has brought back to life.

EASTER TROPARION
FROM THE ORTHODOX TRADITION

Beauty now for ashes wear,
Perfumes for the garb of woe,
Chaplets for dishevelled hair,
Dances for sad footsteps slow;
Open wide your hearts
that they
Let in joy this Easter Day.

GERARD MANLEY HOPKINS